BEARTOOTH COUNTRY

THE ABSAROKA AND BEARTOOTH RANGES

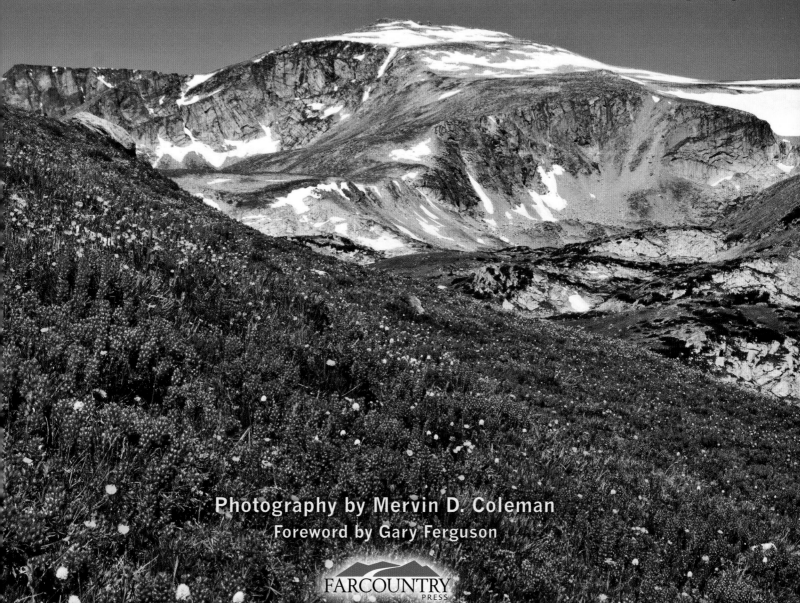

Photography by Mervin D. Coleman
Foreword by Gary Ferguson

FARCOUNTRY
PRESS

Above: A mule deer doe and her two fawns stand in July's rich, green vegetation.
By November there is usually a foot or more of snow on the ground.

Right: A still lake reflects Beartooth Mountain on the Wyoming side of the Beartooth Highway.

Title page: Lupine creates a stark color contrast as 12,204-foot Mount Rearguard looms behind.

Cover: Early morning sun draws bands of light across the faces
of Mount Peale and Mount Hole-in-the-Wall.

Back cover: A mountain goat nanny guides her kid through a meadow. She has begun
to shed her winter coat as the temperatures rise in the high country.

ISBN 10: 1-56037-524-8
ISBN 13: 978-1-56037-524-1

© 2012 by Farcountry Press
Photography © 2012 by Mervin D. Coleman

For more information about our books, write Farcountry Press, P.O. Box 5630, Helena, MT 59604;
call (800) 821-3874; or visit www.farcountrypress.com.

Created, produced, and designed in the United States.
Printed in China.

16   15   14   13   12   1   2   3   4   5

FOREWORD By Gary Ferguson

The enchantment starts a hundred miles out. At that point when travelers, rolling west across the plains of Montana, suddenly glimpse through the windshield the crowns of Beartooth Country announcing themselves on the far horizon—a long, crumpled line of snow-capped peaks shouting into the summer sky. For those

The snow-capped peaks of the Beartooth Range rise behind the green foothills of the Beartooth Front.

unable to resist, who choose to leave the Interstate and make for the Beartooth Highway or the Boulder canyons, or better yet, ditch their car at any of dozens of trailheads and climb atop a horse or shoulder a pack and begin to walk, it's then the love affair begins in earnest. There are paintbrush and lupine and sticky geranium

to be savored, scattered about under the aspen and lodgepole and Douglas-fir. Soon shimmering waterfalls appear, plunging off soaring walls of granite. Then finally, after much climbing, there comes a crossing out of the conifers onto great plates of tundra, 10,000 feet high and then some, stretching on for miles, the whole spectacle washed in buttercups and forget-me-nots, in streamside gardens of scarlet monkeyflowers.

Beartooth Country is a startling place—a nearly incomprehensible geological marvel, a world of wandering animals and swimming fish and soaring birds of prey. Notably, much of the region still possesses nearly its full historic compliment of wildlife—from wolves to wolverines, moose and martens and grizzlies. Besides claiming the magnificent 943,000-acre Absaroka-Beartooth Wilderness, this area is also an integral piece of a larger, 11-million-acre wild landscape stretching west all the way to Idaho, and south through Wyoming past the mighty Tetons. Biologists often refer to this landscape as the largest generally intact ecosystem in the temperate world.

Given the sprawling, dramatic nature of this region, it should come as no surprise that over the decades many have been moved to write about it. Almost without exception those narratives are infused with notions of incredible beauty and sobering ferocity. Indeed, the very first detailed description of the Beartooths (they were then referred to as the Granite Range), written in 1898 by mineralogist James Kimball, contains just such a weave—a blend of scientific wonder and something close to mortal alarm.

Kimball arrived here in early summer of 1898 with a wad of John D. Rockefeller's money in his pocket, charged with creating decent maps of the region, while at the same time keeping an eye out for valuable minerals. One moment we find Kimball writing in his journal like a proper scientist, going on about porphyrite dykes and feldspathic granite, and in the next, offering thoughts well suited to a wide-eyed little boy—astonished by the steep gorges choked with rocks, the ice-formed lakes, the countless waterfalls. Laced through all of it are frequent comments and complaints about "the treacherous weather." That entire summer he was blown and pummeled, turned back time and again from gaining important summits by gale-force winds and pelting hailstorms.

In September, with most but not all of their mapping work completed, Kimball and his men were hit by early snows. They finally managed to struggle back around the Beartooths in October, traveling from Cooke City to the East Rosebud region; their first night in camp they watched in horror as eighty-mile-an-hour winds destroyed their twelve-by-sixteen-foot wall tent, tearing the eyelets out of the fabric and sending clothes, bedding, even the wood stove flying. "Everything had soared away, except blankets under the weight of their possessors," Kimball wrote. "Minor articles, usually worn in pairs, never found their mates. No further adventure proved necessary to force the conviction that endurable conditions for camp life had come to an end for the season."

It shouldn't surprise us that a land like this would produce a kind of determined pluckiness in the people who make their homes along the edges of Beartooth Country. Ranchers, for instance, stung time and again by ferocious storms during spring calving, or having watched their autumn pastures shut down by early snows, have made a fine art out of grinning and bearing it. Even those making their living from tourism have at various times benefited from being hardier than most. For example, when World War II emptied federal bank accounts intended for road maintenance, it meant delays opening the Beartooth Highway, which had been completed in 1936 to connect Red Lodge to Yellowstone National Park. Undeterred by such austerities, in the spring of 1943 a group of locals pooled their money, rented a snowplow, and did the job themselves. The following year, with either money or plows evidently in short supply, the last stretch of the road was opened by nine volunteers from Red Lodge, armed with nothing but snow shovels.

Wildflowers in every color of the rainbow make their brief appearance near Daisy Pass, north of Cooke City, Montana.

In the latter nineteenth century, popular author and pundit Henry George made a claim that hit home with tens of thousands of readers. It didn't really matter, he said, whether or not Americans actually ended up going to the newly created parks and reserves of the West—places like Yellowstone and the surrounding public forests. Simply knowing they exist would engender "a consciousness of freedom." His comments arose in part from the fact that by then Americans had long identified themselves with unfettered landscapes, having claimed across much of history that it was our relationship with such places that forged much of what was most notable about our national character—our hopefulness, our determination, our outgoing nature. At the very least, the thinking went, such wild lands would serve as a kind of spark with which to keep alive essential perspectives—critical thoughts about things like beauty, and wonder, and freedom.

Winter avalanches still roar like freight trains down the steep flanks of Beartooth Country. And every spring, elk continue to climb out of the valleys heading to the tundra, following the rising lines of greening grass. Grizzly bears wander through the high country every fall, bound for some favorite patch of nut-laden whitebark pine. All of which—and a hundred other things besides—make this land even now the stuff of dreams.

Gary Ferguson is the author of nineteen books on science and nature; for more information about his work, visit www.wildwords.net.

Right: A mountain goat munches on summer vegetation as the iconic Bear's Tooth looms in the distance. Crow Indians originally called this spire *Na Piet Say*, which means "the Bear's Tooth."

Far right: The view from the Beartooth Highway, looking northwest into the Absaroka–Beartooth Wilderness. Mirror Lake lies below, while on the skyline above the silhouette of the Bear's Tooth is visible.

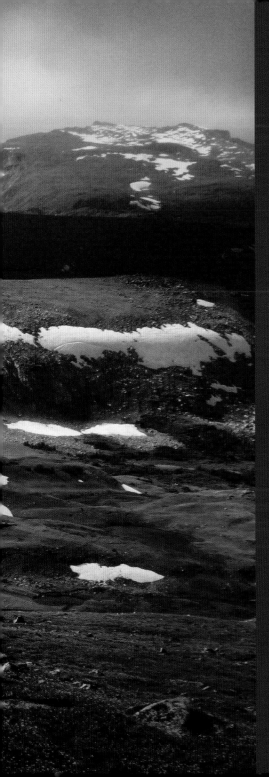

Left: The view from the Beartooth Highway extends for hundreds of miles. Here, snowfields cling to greening plateaus even in July.

Below: A pasque flower makes its short-lived appearance.

Right: Located just a stone's throw from the Beartooth Highway near Cooke City, Montana, the aptly named Crazy Creek has dozens of cascades that visitors can see from the roadway.

Below, left: The view from the West Summit of Beartooth Pass might leave you breathless; the summit exceeds 10,000 feet above sea level.

Below, right: A cutthroat trout's anal fin in detail. Many lakes in the Absaroka–Beartooth Wilderness are teeming with different trout species. The cutthroat is native to the area.

Left: Evening light paints clouds above Beartooth Butte in pink hues, as seen from Clay Butte.

Below: Fireweed, named because it often appears the summer following a forest fire, blossoms near the Clay Butte Lookout Road, north of the Beartooth Highway.

Above: A small lake along the Beartooth Highway starts to thaw. Not until midsummer do snow and ice begin to melt in the high country.

Right: Rock Creek continues to flow during the winter, exhibiting an array of green and blue hues as it makes its way through the mountains and past the town of Red Lodge, Montana.

Above: Riders on horseback cross the West Rosebud River near Roscoe, Montana. Bicycles and motorized vehicles are prohibited in the Absaroka–Beartooth Wilderness.

Left: Trout Lake, near the Northeast Entrance of Yellowstone National Park, is surrounded by lush, green hillsides during the short summer season.

Above, left: A mountain biker navigates rough terrain above the Palisades at Red Lodge Mountain Resort. The resort offers year-round activities for the adventurous.

Above, right: Lenticular clouds over the Beartooth Front signal strong winds in the high country.

Right: The setting sun creates alpine glow, turning this peak a magnificent orange color echoed in Moon Lake's reflection.

Left: East of Livingston, Montana, near Deep Creek, hay bales dot the Western Beartooth foothills as 9,431-foot Elephant Mountain rises in the distance.

Below, left: A bison calf in Yellowstone National Park. Full-grown bull bison can weigh 2,000 pounds.

Below, right: Pilot and Index Peaks provide a dramatic backdrop for the Hancock Ranch just off the Chief Joseph Highway, on the Wyoming side of the Beartooth Highway.

Right: A rainbow forms over Crandall Creek in Wyoming's Sunlight Basin. This area has high populations of grizzly bears and wolves.

Below: Bright–yellow arnica flowers grow in front of a fire-scorched tree near Quinnebaugh Meadows, located up the West Fork of Rock Creek near Red Lodge, Montana.

Above: Waterfalls and cascades are often seen in the Beartooth Range. Here, Arch Waterfall gently tumbles down a rock face.

Left: Island Lake reflects Lonesome Mountain, still covered in patches of snow in early summer. The small circles in the lake are "rise forms"—created when fish eat insects on or just beneath the surface.

Right: Aspen trees glow in yellows and oranges in Rock Creek Canyon, signaling the beginning of a long, cold season ahead.

Below, left: A rugged Beartooth hillside gives one last display of color before winter.

Below, right: Pikas call the high alpine environments of the Beartooth Range home and they live under the snow, subsisting on grasses, lichen, and other vegetation gathered during summer and fall.

Above: Skiers take to the slopes at Red Lodge Mountain Resort. The ski area and surrounding mountains receive more than 200 inches of snow a year.

Left: A full moon rises above the town of Red Lodge.

Above: Rafting on the Stillwater River is a popular summer activity and a great way to experience the Stillwater River Corridor.

Right: A mirrorlike mountain lake reflects Mount Peale and Mount Hole-in-the-Wall at sunrise.

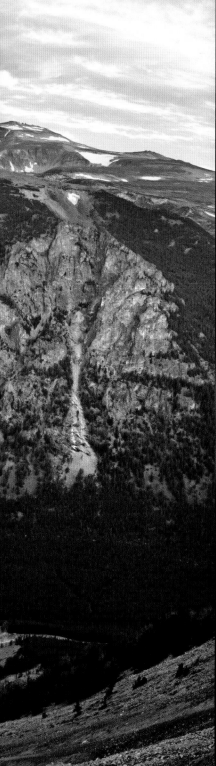

Left: The Beartooth Highway snakes its way up the mountain. Thousands of feet below lies the Rock Creek drainage.

Below, left: Wildflowers adorn the Beartooth Mountains. Here, purple daisies show their colors.

Below, right: Lake Creek Falls thunders its way down the mountain, one of dozens of waterfalls near the Beartooth Highway.

Above, left: Viewed from Rock Creek Canyon, Westminster Spires rises above frosted trees and snow-covered rock.

Above, right: A great horned owl perches in a cottonwood tree.

Right: The Bear's Tooth as seen from Shelf Lake. Climbers normally ascend the spire from the east ridge, seen here at right; the spire is climbed fewer than five times a year.

Above: Paintbrush, named for its bright-red color and brush-like appearance, flourishes throughout Beartooth Country, except in extreme alpine areas.

Left: Twin Lakes at sunset as seen from the Beartooth Highway.

Above: A pronghorn rests near the North Entrance to Yellowstone National Park near Gardiner, Montana.

Right: South of Red Lodge, lupine and sagebrush spread across a valley near Rock Creek Canyon, seen in the distance.

The town of Red Lodge, established in 1884, is considered one of the gateways to Yellowstone National Park by way of the Beartooth Highway.

Above: A snow-covered bison in Yellowstone National Park.

Above, left: The Beartooth Highway, designated a National Scenic Byway in 1989, travels through scenic Custer National Forest.

Facing page: The highest peak in Montana and the Beartooth Range, 12,799-foot Granite Peak was first summited in 1923 by Elers Koch.

Above: Despite the Beartooths' harsh growing conditions, the unique and vibrant bitterroot plant can be found. Adopted as Montana's state flower in 1895, the bitterroot thrives in rocky, mostly dry soil.

Right: Situated in the heart of the Absaroka–Beartooth Wilderness, Spirit Mountain rises behind Black Canyon Lake.

Left: The Beartooth foothills west of Red Lodge provide ample grazing opportunities for cattle.

Below: A bluebird balances on a barbed-wire fence. Known for their electric–blue color, these little birds make a brief appearance in Beartooth Country in the spring before migrating elsewhere.

Above: Natural Bridge Falls, or Boulder Falls, plummets 105 feet and is the main attraction of Natural Bridge State Park and the Boulder River. Picnic areas and a paved trail compliment this unique and beautiful area.

Right: Nestled in dramatic East Rosebud Canyon is East Rosebud Lake.
The elevation change from the lake to the mountaintops is more than 3,500 feet.

Above, left: Heart Mountain, north of the town of Cody, Wyoming, is in the southern Absaroka Range and reaches a height of 8,123 feet.

Above, right: The West Summit of the Beartooth Pass is a whopping 10,000-plus feet above sea level. This switchback is the highest point on the road and offers panoramic views of the plains to the east and the mountains in every other direction.

Left: The many plateaus of the Beartooth Range lose their color as the summer nears its end. Here, rocks and dying vegetation are shown above Gardiner Lake near the top of the Beartooth Highway.

Right: The Yellowstone River winds through the Hayden Valley in Yellowstone National Park.

Below, left: A bull elk surveys his surroundings in a frost-covered field in the Absaroka Range. Montana is home to the largest migratory elk herd in the United States.

Below, right: Two bull bison butt heads during the rut in Yellowstone National Park's Hayden Valley.

Left: Whitetail Peak's north face couloir splits the mountain, tempting skiers and climbers all year long.

Below, left: Moose favor the meadows and marshes of the lower elevations. An adult moose can stand up to seven feet tall and weigh more than 1,000 pounds.

Below, right: Rock Creek, seen here from Meeteetse Bridge, flows even in the coldest of winter weather. Montana's streams are fed almost entirely by winter snowpack.

Above: Participants take to the Beartooth Highway in the annual Beartooth Run, testing their legs and their lungs.

Right: Beartooth Lake casts a reflection of Beartooth Butte. The reddish color on the peak's face is an anomaly in this range, where gray-toned granite is the norm.

Above, left: Lake-at-the-Falls Lake is aptly named. This waterfall, more than 200 feet in height, tumbles loudly down the mountain, adding to the drama.

Above, right: A fly fisherman plies the waters at Rainbow Lake.

Left: Lake-at-the-Falls Lake provides stunning scenery and good fishing.

Above, left: Forget-me-nots live up to their name as their bright-blue color provides a stark contrast to nearby vegetation.

Above, right: A sandhill crane in mid-flight. These birds are found along the Beartooth Front and favor riparian areas with abundant water supplies.

Right: An aerial view of the Beartooth Highway's switchbacks as the road climbs past Gardiner Lake.

Left: Ship Lake with Whitetail Peak on the horizon. This lake, similar to many in the Beartooth Range, is frozen eight months out of the year.

Below, left: Black bears are generally smaller in size than their grizzly bear cousins. Both species' coats can vary in color.

Below, right: Twin mountain goat babies, called kids, stand in a lush meadow.

Right: This idyllic campsite on turquoise Black Canyon Lake is accessible via the Lake Fork of Rock Creek.

Below, left: Two hikers pause to enjoy the view of Rainbow Lake and Beartooth Country.

Below, right: A red squirrel is busy eating and caching food for the coming hard winter.

Above, left: A bighorn sheep ram on winter grounds southwest of Cody, Wyoming. Little snow and an abundance of vegetation make the areas around Cody ideal winter habitat for a variety of animals, including bighorn, elk, pronghorn, and deer.

Above, right: Fall colors in the Clarks Fork Valley of Wyoming as seen from the Chief Joseph Highway.

Left: Long Lake and the Beartooth Highway are accentuated by fall colors.

Above, left: Beartooth Highway usually opens to traffic by Memorial Day each year. Snowplow crews carve through as much as twenty feet of snow.

Above, right: Cooke City, located in northeast Montana, is only accessible via one plowed road in the winter. During this time the town is a haven for snowmobilers and skiers.

Facing page: Skiing in July? You bet! Especially at the Red Lodge International Ski and Snowboard Camp located next to the Beartooth Highway. The area was established in the 1960s and is one of America's oldest ski training grounds.

Above, left: A motorcycle rider takes the curves of the high-elevation Beartooth Highway. Thousands of bikers—motorized or not—ride the pass every year.

Above, right: Woodbine Falls in the Stillwater drainage drops more than 400 feet and was one of the first frozen waterfalls climbed in Montana during the 1970s.

Left: Moon Lake in July. On the horizon is the Bear's Tooth.

Right: Springtime in Beartooth Country is synonymous with green pastures and meadows, such as this meadow and pasture near Luther, Montana, on the eastern edge of the Beartooth Front.

Below, left: Lake Creek Falls as seen from near the Chief Joseph Scenic Highway on the Wyoming side of Beartooth Pass.

Below, right: Touted as the highest bridge in Wyoming, Sunlight Creek Bridge spans Sunlight Creek.

Above, left: Colored rocks in a pool of water. Beauty is everywhere in Beartooth Country, no matter how small.

Above, right: A sunset illuminates clouds over Buffalo Bill Reservoir, located west of Cody, Wyoming. A man-made dam on the Shoshone River creates the reservoir.

Left: Alpenglow transforms this mountain into a red canvas above Glacier Lake on the eastern edge of the Absaroka–Beartooth Wilderness.

Right: Numerous lakes dot the Hellroaring Plateau, accessed from the Rock Creek drainage. Even in summer, snowstorms and freezing temperatures are not uncommon here.

Below, left: Beartooth Falls pours out of Beartooth Lake on the Wyoming side of the Beartooth Highway.

Below, right: Late evening in the Beartooth foothills west of Red Lodge. These foothills offer prime grazing for cattle and wildlife.

Above: A bison defrosts in the morning sun in Yellowstone's Lamar Valley just west of Cooke City, Montana. Temperatures here can drop to 40 below zero during the winter.

Above, left: A grizzly bear walks in the spring snow. Once almost extinct, grizzlies are thriving in Wyoming and Montana, which have the highest populations of the great bear outside Alaska and Canada.

Left: Wolf Mountain and Sawtooth Mountain, located north of Cooke City, both rise above 11,400 feet in elevation.

Mervin D. Coleman has been a professional photographer since 1980, based in Red Lodge, Montana. He owns Coleman Gallery and Studio, which is a portrait studio, framing workshop, and gallery for landscape and nature photography. He worked for the Bureau of Land Management in California and Idaho as a range conservationist. He served in the United States Marine Corps and for more than 4 years and was a reconnaissance systems officer in a RF4 Phantom jet. Coleman's interest in photography has taken him throughout the United State and around the world, including New Zealand, Canada, England, and Italy.

For more information on Coleman, please visit www.mervcoleman.com

Below: July's alpine flowers erupt in blankets of yellows and blues on the Hellroaring Plateau, near the Montana–Wyoming border.

CHRISTY MEDRICK